Sam Willis is a specialist criminal barrister at 5 King's Bench Walk, acting for both prosecution and defence. His practice is focused on serious and complex cases, usually involving violence, weapons, drugs, and fraud.

Prior to his work as a barrister, Sam was an IT developer specialising in mobile applications and data analysis. He is regularly instructed in cases that require a sound technical understanding of digital evidence and the law that applies to it. He has published several mobile apps which are widely used by solicitors and barristers working in criminal law, and he sits on the Bar Council's IT Panel.

A Practical Guide to Digital Communications Evidence in Criminal Law

A Practical Guide to Digital Communications Evidence in Criminal Law

Sam Willis

Barrister

Law Brief Publishing

Published 2023 by Law Brief Publishing, an imprint of Law Brief Publishing Ltd
30 The Parks
Minehead
Somerset
TA24 8BT

www.lawbriefpublishing.com

Paperback: 978-1-914608-74-2

PREFACE

Digital communications evidence is one of the fastest developing areas of criminal justice, impacting most criminal investigations and prosecutions. As a software developer and ardent technophile, I have often found that its use jars with a criminal trial process stuck in the days of envelopes, letters, and stamps.

This book is intended to introduce, summarise, and explore the key forms of digital communications evidence - to assist the reader, practically, to understand, analyse, and present them before judge and jury. It is primarily aimed at junior practitioners, although it should also be of use as a quick reference guide for more senior advocates and litigators. I hope it is helpful.

The law applies to England and Wales, and is believed to be correct as of 2 March 2023.

Sam Willis
March 2023

CONTENTS

GLOSSARY

2G / 3G / 4G / 5G

The different technologies used by mobile telephones to connect to a mobile cellular network, increasing in features and data transfer speeds.

ATTRIBUTION

The process of identifying the user of a particular mobile telephone number.

AZIMUTH

The direction a cell is pointed towards - essentially a compass bearing (0° is due north).

CELL

The equipment used by a mobile network operator to send and receive radio waves as part of a mobile cellular network.

CELL SITE

A physical location where one or more cells have been placed.

CDR

Call Data Records or Call Detail Records (sometimes referred to as billing data) are logs kept by a mobile network operator that hold details about incoming and outgoing telephone calls and other activity using a telephone number.

C P I A

Criminal Procedure and Investigations Act 1996.

D F U

A Digital Forensic Unit is a department, usually within a police force, dedicated to digital forensics.

D M D

A Disclosure Management Document.

E D G E / G P R S / L T E

The different technologies used by mobile telephones to access the internet.

F S R

The Forensic Science Regulator is the independent regulator of forensic science services.

I C C I D

An Integrated Circuit Card Identifier is a number unique to each physical SIM card.

IMEI

An International Mobile Equipment Identity is a number unique to each device that accepts a SIM card (e.g. a mobile telephone).

IMSI

An International Mobile Subscriber Identity is a number stored in the SIM card and uniquely identifies the user.

IPA 2016

Investigatory Powers Act 2016.

IPT

The Investigatory Powers Tribunal is an independent judicial body that investigates complaints made about the use of covert investigative techniques by a public authority.

ISP

An Internet Service Provider is a company providing its customers with access to the internet.

IP ADDRESS

An Internet Protocol Address is a label (in a specific format e.g. 192.168.1.1 or 2001:db8:3333:4444:5555:6666:7777:8888) that identifies a computer device connected to the internet.

M M S

Multimedia Messaging Service allows for the sending of videos and images by a mobile telephone (similar to an SMS text message).

M S I S D N

A Mobile Station International Subscriber Directory Number is the telephone number associated with a SIM card at any particular time.

O I C

The Officer In the Case.

P A C E

Police and Criminal Evidence Act 1984.

R I P A

Regulation of Investigatory Powers Act 2000.

S I M

A Subscriber Identity Module card is a removable card/chip used in a device to allow it to connect to a mobile cellular network.

S M S

Short Message Service allows for the sending of text messages by a mobile telephone.

V P N

A Virtual Private Network is a secure connection, often between two devices, across an unsecured network such as the internet.

W I - F I

A wireless technology used by mobile telephones, laptops, and other computers to access the internet by connecting to a nearby router or access point.

PART ONE

TYPES
OF
EVIDENCE

MOBILE TELEPHONE EXTRACTION

INTRODUCTION

Many modern criminal investigations now involve the seizure of a mobile telephone. Devices range from cheap 'burner' phones with functionality limited to traditional calls and text messages, through to smartphones with a suite of apps providing a wide range of features.

A mobile telephone works with one or more Subscriber Identity Module (SIM) cards, that provide the information necessary for it to register and connect to a mobile cellular network. Every mobile telephone will have a unique identifier – the International Mobile Equipment Identity (IMEI). Devices that accept multiple SIM cards will also have multiple IMEIs.

The volume of information held in modern mobile telephones is staggering. A typical smartphone can hold hundreds of thousands of high-quality photographs, hours of high-resolution video, and years' worth of conversations over traditional SMS text messages, social media, or encrypted messaging apps. A key issue for any criminal investigation is how to collect this information, sift through the vast and varied content, identify anything relevant, and then package it in a form that can be explained and presented.

The focus of this chapter is on the analysis and extraction of data from a mobile telephone. Having seized a mobile telephone from a suspect, investigators can often switch it on and conduct an initial analysis of it – this could involve the investigator scrolling through the text messages on it to identify anything relevant, and then recording those messages in a witness statement.

A further and more detailed analysis of the device requires specialist software and skills. There are three general levels of Mobile Telephone Extraction, which progressively increase in the types of data that can be extracted.

Level 1, also known as logical extraction, is the most common method used. This usually involves connecting the mobile telephone to a computer (often called a 'kiosk') by a cable. Special software on that computer then communicates with the operating system on the mobile telephone and allows it to read the data from it. This is the most straightforward method and allows for the extraction of most types of data (e.g. call logs, contacts, text messages, photos), but will generally only extract items that could have been viewed by simply switching on and scrolling though the mobile telephone.

Level 2, also known as physical extraction, involves a more intensive extraction process usually in a laboratory. This process creates an exact copy of the mobile telephone's memory, rather than accessing and extracting information item by item. This often allows for deleted data to be recovered.

Level 3 involves the use of an expert undertaking a specialist examination of the device. This is often required for devices that are damaged and so a Level 1 or 2 extraction will not work, or where there are other specialist issues that can only be addressed by an expert.

LAW AND GUIDANCE

Police constables have various statutory powers under the Police and Criminal Evidence Act 1984 (PACE) to seize items, including mobile telephones.

Section 8(2) of PACE allows for the seizure of items found during a search carried out with a warrant.

Section 18(2) of PACE allows for the seizure of items found during a search of premises occupied or controlled by a person under arrest for an indictable offence.

Section 19 of PACE allows for the seizure of items where the constable is lawfully on any premises.

Sections 19(4) and 20 of PACE extend those three powers by including a power to require any information stored in any electronic form contained in a computer and accessible from the premises to be produced in a form in which it can be taken away and in which it is visible and legible.

Section 32(9) of PACE allows for the seizure of items found during the search of a person under arrest.

Sections 50 and 51 of the Criminal Justice and Police Act 2001 extend the above powers under PACE to cover circumstances where it is not reasonably practicable to separate material that can be lawfully seized from other material.

There are other similar powers of seizure for other law enforcement agencies (e.g. for immigration officers under section 28G of the Immigration Act 1971).

Although it is not expressly provided for in the statutory powers listed above, the courts appear to have accepted that a power to extract and examine material from a seized mobile telephone flows from these general powers (for examples, see *R (Cabot Global Ltd) v Barkingside Magistrates' Court* [2015] EWHC 1458 (Admin), *R (Faisaltex Ltd) v Crown Court at Preston* [2008] EWHC 2832 (Admin), and *R (A and another) v Central Criminal Court* [2017] EWHC 70 (Admin)).

Various other documents provide guidance on how investigators should deal with mobile telephones.

Despite having been drafted over 10 years ago, the 'ACPO Good Practice Guidelines for Digital Evidence' are still frequently cited by law enforcement authorities. They set out the following four principles that should be followed:

Principle 1: No action taken by law enforcement agencies, persons employed within those agencies or their agents should change data which may subsequently be relied upon in court.

Principle 2: In circumstances where a person finds it necessary to access original data, that person must be competent to do so and be able to give evidence explaining the relevance and the implications of their actions.

Principle 3: An audit trail or other record of all processes applied to digital evidence should be created and preserved. An independent third party should be able to examine those processes and achieve the same result.

Principle 4: The person in charge of the investigation has overall responsibility for ensuring that the law and these principles are adhered to.

The 'Forensic Science Regulator Codes of Practice and Conduct' also set out minimum standards to be followed by those conducting forensic examinations of mobile telephones.

USES

The data extracted from a mobile telephone often helps paint a vivid picture of contact between parties. Call logs record incoming and outgoing telephone calls, including date, time, and duration. Message and chat logs record conversations, including the actual content of messages alongside date and timestamps (with the caveat that some messages may have been deleted, depending on the method of extraction). Address book entries show links to other individuals and other telephone numbers, and can often provide other useful information such as nicknames and relationships.

Although the focus of this book is on communications evidence, modern mobile telephones can often be a treasure trove of other information relevant to an investigation. Examples of this include browser history, photographs, videos, stored account details, and files.

LIMITATIONS

The main limitations for each level of extraction are set out above. As the level increases, so does the time and cost. This inevitably involves an assessment of proportionality when identifying the appropriate level of extraction in any particular investigation.

Modern smartphones come with built-in encryption, which essentially scrambles the data on the device until the correct password is entered. Some extraction software products can bypass this protection, depending on the make and model of mobile telephone. There is a game of 'cat and mouse' as a software company manages to bypass or break the encryption for one model of mobile telephone, only for the manufacturer to fix it for the next model.

Software companies must also constantly update their extraction software, as new models of mobile telephones are released and applications running on those devices are changed. If a new social media platform becomes popular, the software running on a 'kiosk' has to be updated so that it can access the material on that particular platform's app.

The deletion of material is another issue. Most modern smartphones can be remotely wiped – an owner can send a signal to the device that it receives when it next connects to the internet, triggering it to delete its content. Investigators must be careful not to inadvertently allow the device to connect to the internet for this reason. Similarly, some social media and messaging apps allow for messages received by a device to be remotely wiped by the sender or automatically deleted after a set time. This creates an obvious challenge when a mobile telephone is later analysed, and may be a situation where a Level 2 or 3 extraction is required.

PRESENTATION

The physical product created at the end of the extraction process will very much depend upon the level of extraction, the type of device interrogated, and the specific extraction software used. However, generally an archive file will be produced (a compressed folder containing the extracted data). These tend to be very large files which require special software to access and are therefore not very useful for sharing with others – either as used or unused material.

Investigators can create a PDF report from these archives, which sets out the extracted data in a form that can be shared more easily. This PDF report can contain all the data extracted, or can be a subset of the data (e.g. only messages, or only messages between two dates, or only messages selected by the investigator). It is this PDF report which is typically served as evidence or disclosed. It is possible for one PDF report to be generated containing the data said to be relied upon as evidence (e.g. all of the SMS text messages) and another PDF report to be generated containing every item of data extracted, to be scheduled and considered for disclosure – whether or not it is fair to sub-divide the evidence in this way will be fact-specific, and should not be done in a case where it is necessary for all of the data to be exhibited so that the parts on which the prosecution rely can fairly be seen in their proper context (see *Lord Chancellor v SVS Solicitors* [2017] EWHC 1045 (QB)).

There are often requests made, both by those prosecuting and defending, for a 'full download' of a mobile telephone to be provided by investigators. This term is vague and imprecise – it could be a request for a PDF report containing all the data extracted rather than just a subset, or it could be a request for the archive file accompanied by the special software required to open it. Often its use simply comes from a misunderstanding of the extraction process, what data is available, and in what format. A request should instead be specific as to the type of material (e.g. all content extracted, or just SMS text messages), the format (e.g. a PDF report) and any other parameters (e.g. date range).

At trial, evidence extracted from mobile telephones is often presented within a 'working document' communications schedule (for calls logs and messages) or as part of an Agreed Facts document. For example:

- *The data on the seized mobile telephone was extracted. The following SMS text messages had been sent and received on that device, using the telephone number 0131 496 xxxx:*

Date	Time	Sender	Recipient	Content
5 December 2022	23:15:34	07700 900xxx (Clive)	0131 496 xxxx	Hv u got any w
5 December 2022	23:15:58	0131 496 xxxx	07700 900xxx (Clive)	Yh
5 December 2022	23:26:00	0131 496 xxxx	07700 900xxx (Clive)	1 hour

Date	Time	Sender	Recipient	Content
5 December 2022	23:54:12	07700 900xxx (Clive)	0131 496 xxxx	Ok usual place
6 December 2022	00:05:03	07700 900xxx (Clive)	0131 496 xxxx	Here
6 December 2022	01:04:43	0131 496 xxxx	07700 900xxx (Clive)	Coming – got 5 w

FUTURE DEVELOPMENTS

The increasing reliance on mobile telephones in everyday life is likely to continue, resulting in even more information being stored on them. This in turn generates a significant burden on investigators who have to sift through the extracted material and identify anything of relevance. The use of artificial intelligence (software that learns and adapts by itself, that could be used to accurately identify relevant data) may assist with this but the technology is still some way off from being able to replace a trained investigator spending hours looking through material extracted from multiple mobile telephones.

There is also a general move by technology companies (e.g. mobile telephone manufacturers) towards more secure encryption, and there is an ongoing debate over the balance between the right to privacy and the need for law enforcement to have access to some communications. This is likely to be a source of further legislation over the coming decade.

SIM CARD
EXTRACTION

INTRODUCTION

A SIM card is a small removable memory chip inserted into a mobile device to allow it to register and connect to a mobile cellular network. Provided by mobile network operators, they are mostly used with mobile telephones but can also be found in a wide range of other devices such as tablet computers, laptops, vehicles, and even automatic gates / garage doors. Each device typically has a slot for one SIM card, though some modern devices have multiple SIM card slots (typically called Dual-SIM or Multi-SIM devices).

SIM cards are typically made of PVC and have a small rectangular contact plate. They come in one of three sizes depending on the device that they are intended for: Standard, Micro, or Nano. Despite the name, the Standard size is now rare and most modern devices only use the Nano size of SIM card. Each physical SIM card is identified by a unique number, called an Integrated Circuit Card Identifier (ICCID).

A SIM card is essentially a memory card. Its primary purpose is to store the key pieces of data used by a device to connect to a mobile cellular network: an International Mobile Subscriber Identity (IMSI), which is a number uniquely identifying the user of the SIM card, and a Mobile Station International Subscriber Directory Number (MSISDN), which is essentially the telephone number associated to that SIM card.

Some devices, particularly older mobile telephones, also use the SIM card's memory to store other information such as 'address book' contacts (name and number pairs) and SMS text messages. Most modern devices do not do this and instead store information in the device's internal memory.

The process used by investigators to extract data from a SIM card is broadly the same as it is for Mobile Telephone Extraction (the same extraction software will usually read data from both the mobile device and any SIM card inserted into the device). A SIM card can also be directly inserted into a SIM card reader and accessed separately.

LAW AND GUIDANCE

The applicable law for this type of evidence is the same as it is for Mobile Telephone Extraction.

USES

A SIM card is often extracted to identify the mobile telephone number associated with it. From there, a Subscriber Check can be carried out and Call Data Records can be obtained.

The other reason to extract data from a SIM card is to obtain any contacts or SMS text messages stored on it. Having access to stored contacts can evidence associations between individuals, as well as identifying nicknames. Having access to SMS text messages has the obvious use of showing the actual communications between individuals.

LIMITATIONS

The data stored on a SIM card is quite limited, and so they tend to offer few investigatory leads. Modern devices do not use them to store contact information or SMS text messages, instead using the device's internal storage. Even with older devices that do use them as storage, the available space tends to be just 256KB (typically enough for 250 contacts or 32 SMS text messages).

It is also possible to protect a SIM card with a PIN code, though this feature is rarely used (this is different from the use of a PIN code to protect a mobile device itself, which is far more common). If set, this can prevent extraction software (and any mobile device) from reading the data on the SIM card without the correct PIN code.

PRESENTATION

Evidence extracted from a SIM card is usually provided either: (a) as part of a PDF report, as with a Mobile Telephone Extraction, or (b) set out in the body of a witness statement from the individual who performed the extraction.

Given the limited volume of data often obtained, this type of evidence is typically presented at trial in a table within an Agreed Facts document. For example:

- *The data on the seized SIM card was extracted and examined. The following contacts had been saved on the SIM card:*

Contact Name	*Contact Number*
Girlfriend	*07700 900xxx*
Dave Smith	*08081 570xxx*
John Doe	*0131 496 xxxx*
Jane Doe	*07700 900xxx*

FUTURE DEVELOPMENTS

It is likely that in the next few years physical SIM cards will be replaced with eSIMs (Embedded-SIMs). Rather than being a physical chip sent out by a mobile network operator and inserted into the device, these are not removable and are permanently embedded within the device. The data stored on the eSIM is programmable and can be updated remotely by a mobile network operator – meaning that if the user changes network provider, the data on the eSIM is simply updated by the new operator, rather than a replacement physical SIM card being sent out.

CALL DATA RECORDS

INTRODUCTION

Call Data Records (also known as Call Detail Records) are logs kept by a mobile network operator that hold details about incoming and outgoing telephone calls and other activity using one of its telephone numbers. These logs are primarily kept for the purposes of billing – they allow the company to calculate how many minutes of calls have been made and how many text messages have been sent (hence why they are sometimes referred to as billing data). Data sessions are also recorded where the telephone number has been used to connect to the internet.

An individual Call Data Record typically contains the type of contact (e.g. telephone call, SMS text message), the telephone number of the caller/sender, the telephone number of the receiver, the date and time of the call/message, the duration of call, the result (e.g. call connected, forwarded to voicemail), and the IMEI of the mobile telephone used (by comparing this to the IMEIs of seized mobile telephones, investigators can identify the device that was being used at the time of the record). Data session records tend to record the session's date, start time, duration, amount of data that was sent or received, and the IMEI of the mobile telephone used.

Call Data Records are obtained by a request to the relevant mobile network operator, who then provide them. They are usually sent in both PDF and spreadsheet format. Individual files are provided for each telephone number requested, and each file contains a table with the rows representing individual Call Data Records. The spreadsheet format has the advantage of being easily searchable and filterable – it is also the format required by most experts instructed to analyse the data as it can be imported into specialist software.

LAW AND GUIDANCE

Part 3 of the Investigatory Powers Act 2016 (IPA 2016) provides the legal framework for the obtaining of Call Data Records.

Sections 60A-61A provide several ways that a public authority can be authorised to access data from a telecommunications system.

For the purposes of Part 3, a public authority is either one of the listed organisations in the table at Schedule 4 or a local authority.

Under section 60A, the Investigatory Powers Commissioner can grant the authorisation. Under sections 61 and 61A, a designated senior officer within the public authority itself can grant the authorisation. The meaning of "designated senior officer" is set out in the table at Schedule 4 for each listed organisation.

Sections 60A-61A all state that an authorisation can only be granted if it is necessary to obtain the data for one of a list of reasons, and all three sections include "the applicable crime purpose" as one of those possible reasons, defined as:

(a)   *where the communications data is wholly or partly events data, the purpose of preventing or detecting serious crime;*

(b)   *in any other case, the purpose of preventing or detecting crime or of preventing disorder.*

Section 261 provides various definitions, including for "entity data" and "events data".

Call Data Records fall within "events data", and so obtaining them must be necessary to prevent or detect serious crime.

Section 263 defines "serious crime" as:

(a)   the offence, or one of the offences, which is or would be
constituted by the conduct concerned is an offence for which a
person who has reached the age of 18 (or, in relation to Scotland
or Northern Ireland, 21) and has no previous convictions could
reasonably be expected to be sentenced to imprisonment for a
term of 3 years or more, or (b) the conduct involves the use of
violence, results in substantial financial gain or is conduct by a
large number of persons in pursuit of a common purpose

In addition to the statute, the 'Communications Data Code of Practice' provides guidance on the use of powers under the IPA 2016.

The 'Federation of Communication Services UK Standard for CDRs' specifies the format that mobile network operators should provide the Call Data Records in (to ensure consistency).

USES

In a criminal investigation these records can provide a wealth of information – they can evidence that a specific contact was made (e.g. to support an assertion that a telephone call was made at a specific time), they can show general patterns of contact (e.g. by showing frequent and repeated contact from one telephone number to another), and they can provide new investigative leads (e.g. by identifying frequent contact with a telephone number unknown to the investigation). These records also provide the underlying data for Cell Site Evidence, covered in a separate chapter.

The absence of Call Data Records at a particular time can often also provide compelling evidence. If the records show regular calls, text messages and data sessions in the hours before and after a particular event, but none at all during it, this may imply that the user deliberately did not use their mobile telephone for that period – because they had some involvement in or knowledge of the offence.

LIMITATIONS

Call Data Records only establish contact between two telephone numbers – other evidence is required to establish the identities of the individuals using those telephone numbers during that particular contact.

Although Call Data Records can show that a telephone call was made or that a text message was sent, they cannot provide the content of the call or message. For data sessions, the records merely show that a connection to the internet had been established – they do not show what was done using that connection and so cannot be used to identify which apps had been used or which websites were browsed. This means that video calls and voice calls made over the internet (a standard feature on many social media platforms) do not appear in the Call Data Records. If a user was browsing the internet and then sent an email, these two activities could be captured in the same record rather than each activity triggering its own.

A further limitation for data session records is that a mobile telephone can be constantly connected to the internet and using data without any user interaction. A modern smartphone will frequently connect to the internet to check for updates and to backup data, all without the owner necessarily being anywhere near it.

Call Data Records are also generally only held by a mobile network operator for 12 months, so investigators must obtain them before they are deleted.

PRESENTATION

At trial the contents of the files containing the Call Data Records are usually combined into a 'working document' communications schedule. These contain the most useful parts of a Call Data Record (type of contact, initiating telephone number, receiving telephone number, duration, outcome) but are also colour-coded. Each row is numbered, for ease of reference, and each individual is assigned a unique colour which is then used to highlight all the telephone numbers in the schedule that have been attributed to that individual.

A second common presentation method is the use of association charts. These 'spider's web'-style diagrams show the volume of telephone calls and other events between the key telephone numbers identified in an investigation. They are particularly useful in conspiracy cases to show unusual levels of communication between suspects (e.g. to show frequent contact between individuals in the lead up to, during, and immediately after an offence).

FUTURE DEVELOPMENTS

Many social media and other communication apps now allow users to make voice and video calls to each other. These cannot be seen on the Call Data Records as they appear within a data session rather than as a traditional telephone call. The value of standard Call Data Records in criminal investigations may be diminished if more users switch to using these types of services.

SUBSCRIBER
CHECKS

INTRODUCTION

As with Call Data Records, mobile network operators also keep records of who a telephone number is assigned to.

A Subscriber Check is made by a request to the relevant mobile network operator, who then provide any subscriber details they have about that specific telephone number. The response is usually contained within a PDF file, one file per telephone number. The details provided typically include: first name, last name, date of birth, address, email address, the registration date and time of that telephone number, the activation date and time of that telephone number, and the first network connection date and time of that telephone number.

LAW AND GUIDANCE

Part 3 of the IPA 2016 provides the legal framework for the use of Subscriber Checks.

Sections 60A-61A provide several ways that a public authority can be authorised to access data from a telecommunications system.

For the purposes of Part 3, a public authority is either one of the listed organisations in the table at Schedule 4 or a local authority.

Under section 60A, the Investigatory Powers Commissioner can grant the authorisation. Under sections 61 and 61A, a designated senior officer within the public authority itself can grant the authorisation. The meaning of "designated senior officer" is set out in the table at Schedule 4 for each listed organisation.

Sections 60A-61A all state that an authorisation can only be granted if it is necessary to obtain the data for one of a list of reasons, and all three sections include "the applicable crime purpose" as one of those possible reasons, defined as:

> (a)   where the communications data is wholly or partly events data, the purpose of preventing or detecting serious crime;

> (b)   in any other case, the purpose of preventing or detecting crime or of preventing disorder.

Section 261 provides various definitions, including for "entity data" and "events data".

The information covered by a Subscriber Check falls within "entity data" and so obtaining the data must be necessary to prevent or detect crime or to prevent disorder.

In addition to the statute, the 'Communications Data Code of Practice' provides guidance on the use of powers under the IPA 2016.

USES

Attribution is the principal use of a Subscriber Check. Investigators can identify the details of the individual that 'owns' a particular telephone number.

LIMITATIONS

A Subscriber Check can only identify the individual that 'owns' a telephone number – it cannot tell who was actually using it at any given time, and it is easy for mobile telephones and SIM cards to be temporarily used by others or borrowed.

There are also many telephone numbers in use that are 'unregistered'. These are usually on a Pay As You Go model (users 'top-up' the credit used to make telephone calls and send text messages, rather than having an ongoing monthly subscription). These often will not have any subscriber details assigned to them unless the user has actively registered their details with the mobile network operator.

PRESENTATION

The results of Subscriber Checks are typically presented at trial within an Agreed Facts document.

FUTURE DEVELOPMENTS

A small number of countries around the world still allow unregistered SIM cards to be purchased – the United Kingdom is one of them. The trend has been towards mandatory registration, with some countries requiring identification documents to be shown and biometric information to be taken. It is possible that the UK will move to such a model in the future, which would make identifying the individual who 'owns' the telephone number easier.

CELL SITE EVIDENCE

INTRODUCTION

Cell Site Evidence is essentially the application of geography to Call Data Records – using information within the records to calculate the area that a mobile telephone has been in.

When a mobile telephone makes or receives a telephone call or SMS text message, or is connected to the internet (not using Wi-Fi), it is connected to the mobile cellular network using radio waves sent between it and a cell (the equipment used to send and receive the radio waves). There is a network of these cells dotted around the country, owned and maintained by four of the large mobile network operators. Often several cells are located at one physical location, called a cell site, with the cells pointed in different directions to achieve the best coverage. There are various types of cell sites, from dedicated radio masts to micro cells situated on the sides of buildings. The direction that a particular cell is pointed towards is called the azimuth – essentially a compass bearing (0° is due north). The coverage of an individual cell varies, depending on various geographical and technical factors. The range of a cell can vary from around 500m up to 35km, and coverage often overlaps so that multiple cells serve the same location. A mobile telephone will typically use the cell with the strongest signal, but this depends on various factors including how many users are already using that cell.

As well as recording some information about the type of communication made, a Call Data Record also contains details about the cells used. The records typically contain an identifying code for the cell, the address of the cell site, and the azimuth of the cell. For telephone calls the records contain details for both the first used and last used cells during that call.

This information can then be analysed, typically by plotting the cell site positions. This is usually done using special software that imports the Call Data Records from the spreadsheet files provided by the mobile network operator and plots them on a map. It is important to note that the point plotted does not represent where the mobile telephone was – it merely means that the mobile telephone was somewhere within the service area of the cell located at that point.

It is often important for an investigation to determine if a particular location is within the service area of a particular cell. For example, in a burglary case it may be crucial to know if the burgled address was within the service area of the cell the suspect's mobile telephone was using at the time of the offence. The fact that the cell site is relatively nearby is often insufficient – because the power of the cell used and obstructions such as trees, hills and buildings will impact on both the shape and range of the cell's service area. It is for this reason that a location survey is carried out. This involves taking special equipment to the location, which then records the cells that provide service there. The results are then analysed to see if the cell the mobile telephone was connected to was one of the cells that provided service to the location surveyed.

LAW AND GUIDANCE

The law relating to the acquisition of the underlying Call Data Records is dealt with in an earlier chapter.

Litigation regarding the use of Cell Site Evidence has focused on the limits of non-expert evidence.

In *R v Calland* [2017] EWCA Crim 2308, the Court of Appeal heard a prosecution appeal against a terminatory ruling. The trial judge had excluded Cell Site Evidence where there had been no location survey and the prosecution "wished the jury to make the assumption that because the [relevant telephone] made a call routed through a particular mast, and because [the defendant] was at the relevant time in proximity to that mast and had a phone, he must therefore have been using the [relevant telephone] when he was observed [by police officers]". The appeal was refused, with the Court of Appeal stating:

> *If the prosecution wished to follow that line, they could and should have obtained appropriate expert evidence so that the jury might permissibly have drawn a proper inference. The judge, in our view rightly, foresaw the danger that if the case were presented as the prosecution would wish it to be, the jury would be drawn into making a speculative assumption for which there was no evidential foundation.*

In *R v Turner* [2020] EWCA Crim 1241, the Court of Appeal heard an appeal against conviction where the prosecution had relied upon 'top cells' analysis (which identifies the most frequently used cells over a period) and maps produced by an analyst. The appeal was refused, with the court finding that:

> *[the analyst] clearly has considerable experience in assembling and portraying call data evidence for the purposes of supporting the attribution of a phone to a specific person. However, the analysis she performed does not require any particular expertise or experience which is the hallmark of an expert in this context and she was not put forward as an expert witness. In her evidence, she made expressly clear that she was not an expert witness: she said she was a professional witness who simply analysed data which she then set out in a report... on the basis that the top mast for a particular number may "give an indication of where the user might live"... We find nothing wrong with that description of her proper function.*

The courts have therefore accepted that some types of Cell Site Evidence can be relied upon without the need for an expert witness to be instructed, whereas other types, particularly where a party seeks to show that a mobile telephone was in a specific location (as opposed to a general area), will require opinion evidence from a suitably qualified expert. It should be noted that it is common for the prosecution to instruct a non-expert analyst at the outset of a case to produce maps, which are then later adopted by an expert instructed as the case progresses to trial.

Guidance in relation to the analysis of Cell Site Evidence has been published by the Forensic Science Regulator (FSR). The 'Codes of Practice and Conduct, Appendix: Digital Forensics – Cell Site Analysis' sets standards that should be followed by all forensic science providers dealing with Cell Site Evidence.

USES

Cell Site Evidence is useful for identifying the general area that a mobile telephone was in. This is particularly relevant in cases where an individual has travelled to a location in order to commit an offence and the analysis reveals that their mobile telephone was in the general area of the offence at the relevant time.

The general movement of a mobile telephone can also be tracked by analysing the Cell Site Evidence. As a mobile telephone travels it will connect to new cells along the way. If these are captured in the Call Data Records (e.g. if the user is making telephone calls, sending text messages, or is connected to the internet during that travel), then a map plotting the cells will reveal that travel.

The attribution of a particular mobile telephone number to a specific individual can also be assisted with Cell Site Evidence. Movement of the mobile telephone can be compelling if tied to other evidence that reveals the individual making that journey – such as surveillance or Automatic Number Plate Recognition records. A 'bed and breakfast' analysis involves looking at the most frequently used cells over a period, when the device is used for the first time and the last time each day – relying on the fact that most people take their mobile telephone home with them to charge. This then reveals the general area that the mobile telephone's user lives in. Similarly, a 'top cells' analysis identifies the most frequently used cells over a period – again, revealing the rough area that the mobile telephone is mostly used in. Co-location is another method of attribution, which compares the Call Data Records of two separate mobile telephone numbers. If the two mobile telephones have frequently used cells at similar times in similar locations, it can be inferred that they were together – and possibly in use by the same person.

LIMITATIONS

It is important to understand that Cell Site Evidence cannot pinpoint the precise location of a mobile telephone. It can only show that a mobile telephone was in the coverage area of a particular cell at a particular time, and following a location survey it may be able to determine that a particular location of interest was within that coverage area.

As with Call Data Records, Cell Site Evidence can only establish that a particular mobile telephone was connected to a particular cell – it cannot identify the individual that had possession of that mobile telephone (though as above, some analysis such as 'bed and breakfast' can provide support for the general attribution of a telephone number to an individual).

It is also possible for cells to be moved by the mobile network operators, particularly where they are installed temporarily to deal with increased demand. This can cause issues where there has been a delay in conducting a location survey, as the results will no longer show the coverage that existed at the time of the offence.

The timings of telephone calls and other records (e.g. SMS text messages) can be relied upon for the purposes of Cell Site Evidence, but this is not necessarily the case for data session records – great care must be taken with these. This is because data sessions tend to be permanent and persistent connections, rather than representing a one-off event like a telephone call. Generally, a new Call Data Record will be generated for a data session when the mobile telephone initiates a new session or when the cell in use changes for an existing session – but this is not always the case, and it is possible for a mobile telephone to move cells within a small area, whilst connected to the internet, without the change being logged. There are other circumstances where a new record will be generated without anything necessarily happening to the mobile telephone – this could be because the billing system detects that a certain volume of data has been used or that the connection has been live for a certain length of time. In these cases, a new record is generated that uses the last-known (cached or stored) cell details. It is therefore usually only possible to say that the mobile telephone was connected to that cell at or before the time given in the record, but after the time of the last data session that was using a different cell. An expert is usually required to specifically address these sorts of issues when data session records are being relied upon, because it is a very technical area that can lead to serious injustice if not properly handled.

In *R v Calland* (cited above), the Court of Appeal set out some of the technical limitations of Cell Site Evidence:

> *Such expert evidence often explains that mobile phones masts may be angled in one direction but not another and that the range and extent of coverage varies from cell site to cell site and may be affected by topographical features such as hills or tall buildings. Expert evidence often also explains that a mobile phone making a call in a particular location may be served by more than one cell site and the question may therefore arise as to which of the relevant sites provided the strongest signal and was most likely to have transmitted a call from that location.*

PRESENTATION

Analyses such as 'bed and breakfast' attribution and 'top cells' are typically carried out by an analyst and contained within a witness statement. These are then often presented at trial in an Agreed Facts document.

Analysis involving mapping is either carried out by an analyst or a cell site expert witness. The usual process is for an explanatory witness statement (by the analyst) or a written expert report (by the cell site expert) to be produced, accompanied by a set of maps. At trial these are typically printed out on A3 paper and given to the jury, with the analyst or expert witness called live to explain them.

Due to the technical nature of Cell Site Evidence, a slideshow presentation or video explaining the key concepts is often provided by a cell site expert which is then shown to the jury during the trial.

FUTURE DEVELOPMENTS

An area ripe for improvement is the presentation of Cell Site Evidence at trial. Jurors are now often shown a slideshow presentation or video which explains the key concepts, but the established method of printing bundles of maps and going through them is tricky to present and difficult for juries to understand. Using videos, diagrams, and other interactive material in addition to printed maps is a potential future development.

IP ADDRESS RESOLUTION

INTRODUCTION

An Internet Protocol (IP) address is a unique identifier for a device connected to the internet. As will be seen later in this chapter, for most households this device is the router provided by an Internet Service Provider (ISP) so that multiple devices can connect to the internet (both wired and using Wi-Fi).

An IP address allows the flow of data to and from a device by identifying it, akin to how a street address is used to identify the intended destination of a letter.

Examples of investigations involving IP addresses include where communications have been sent over social media or email, or where illegal material has been accessed using the internet. In such cases, investigators seek to obtain the IP address used to send the communication or access the material. The provider that was used to send the communication or host the material (e.g. social media platforms, file storage services, email hosts) can be asked to provide the IP address that was used to access their platform by a specific account at a specific time.

Once the IP address has been obtained, the relevant ISP can be asked to provide the details of the customer that was assigned that IP address at the relevant time. This process is called IP Address Resolution.

LAW AND GUIDANCE

Part 3 of the IPA 2016 provides the legal framework for the use of IP Address Resolution (which falls under the definition of "internet connection records").

Sections 60A-61A provide several ways that a public authority can be authorised to access internet connection records from a telecommunications system.

For the purposes of Part 3, a public authority is one of the listed organisations in the table at Schedule 4 (a local authority is excluded from obtaining internet connection records by section 62).

Under section 60A, the Investigatory Powers Commissioner can grant the authorisation. Under sections 61 and 61A, a designated senior officer within the public authority itself can grant the authorisation. The meaning of "designated senior officer" is set out in the table at Schedule 4 for each listed organisation.

Sections 60A-61A all state that an authorisation can only be granted if it is necessary to obtain the data for one of a list of reasons, and all three sections include "the applicable crime purpose", defined as:

(a) *where the communications data is wholly or partly events data, the purpose of preventing or detecting serious crime;*

(b) *in any other case, the purpose of preventing or detecting crime or of preventing disorder.*

Section 261 provides various definitions, including for "entity data" and "events data". IP Address Resolution, where an investigator wants to know the identity of a person using an IP address at a specific time and date, will be an application for entity data. This means that obtaining the data must be necessary to prevent or detect crime or to prevent disorder.

Section 62 provides further specific restrictions on the use of internet connection records. The additional condition ("Condition A") in section 62(3) is the most applicable to IP Address Resolution, which means that obtaining the data must also be necessary:

> *to identify which person or apparatus is using an internet service where—*
>
> (a) *the service and time of use are already known, but*
>
> (b) *the identity of the person or apparatus using the service is not known.*

There are further restrictions in section 62 that apply to other types of requests for internet connection records (e.g. where the identity of a person is already known but the request is for data to show what online services they had accessed).

In addition to the statute, Part 9 of the 'Communications Data Code of Practice' provides guidance specific to IP Address Resolution under the IPA 2016.

USES

Identification is the principal use of IP Address Resolution. Investigators can identify, subject to various limitations, details of the individual using an IP address.

LIMITATIONS

Identification is only possible once the IP address and activity time are both known. This initial stage can be difficult and time consuming. Providers based abroad may also be unwilling or unable (due to the laws in their host jurisdiction) to provide the required details.

It is imperative that the activity time is accurate. This is because most IP addresses are not permanently assigned to a customer – they frequently change, a new IP address being assigned from a 'pool' of available addresses. A specific IP address may therefore be assigned to customer A at 10:00am but assigned to customer B by 10:30am.

It should also be noted that this process can only provide the details of the ISP's customer – this is not necessarily the individual that actually sent the communication or accessed the material. In cases of publicly available hotspots (e.g. free Wi-Fi in a coffee shop), the customer will be the business providing that access. Similarly, most homes have a router which shares one IP address with many devices connected to the internet, some using Wi-Fi and some plugged in using Ethernet cables. The customer will be the individual that has the contract with the ISP, but multiple individuals may have access to the internet through that router. To adopt the earlier letter analogy, the street address can be obtained but not the name of the intended recipient. It follows that devices are often easier to identify when they are not connected to a router sharing one IP address with many devices, such as when a mobile telephone is connected to the internet using the mobile cellular network rather than using Wi-Fi.

Finally, it is possible for a user to hide their IP address using a Virtual Private Network (VPN). These services allow a user to create a secure, encrypted 'tunnel' from their device to a VPN host device anywhere else in the world. When the user then sends a communication or accesses material over the internet, the data is transmitted through this 'tunnel'. The effect is that the VPN host device's IP address is used, rather than that of the user's own device. It may then be impossible to ascertain the user's actual IP address.

PRESENTATION

Customer details obtained from IP Address Resolution are usually set out in the body of a witness statement from an individual employed by the relevant ISP.

At trial, evidence obtained by IP Address Resolution is typically presented within an Agreed Facts document.

FUTURE DEVELOPMENTS

Over the last decade the number of devices able to connect to the internet has grown exponentially. Many modern household appliances and devices (e.g. fridges, coffee machines, light bulbs, vacuum cleaners) now have features requiring an internet connection. It is therefore becoming harder for investigators to identify precisely which device in a property, identified through IP Address Resolution, might have been used. As an extreme example, there are now models of fridge freezers which can be used to browse the internet, download material, and post on social media sites.

The methods of connecting to the internet are also changing. In decades gone, the internet was mostly accessed through a physical landline connection to a property. Households are now able to access the internet through the mobile telephone network and satellite connections, with other technologies being trialled (e.g. using lasers and a network of helium balloons). The criminal justice system will need to keep on top of these developments

INTERCEPT
MATERIAL

INTRODUCTION

In the UK, intercept material (traditionally thought of as 'phone-tapping' i.e. listening to and recording a live telephone call) can generally only be used for intelligence purposes – it cannot be used evidentially in court proceedings. This prohibition is unique within Europe and has been in place (imposed by various statutes) since 1985. The justification is operational secrecy – the need to limit how much is publicly known about the capabilities of the law enforcement authorities. However, there are several categories of intercept evidence which do not fall within the prohibition and so can be used evidentially – these are addressed in the following chapters.

LAW AND GUIDANCE

The law on intercept material is now contained within the IPA 2016.

Part 1 of that Act makes it a criminal offence to unlawfully intercept communications.

Part 2 sets out circumstances when intercepting communications will be lawful. These include using warrants (e.g. a targeted interception warrant or a targeted equipment interference warrant) and where a statutory exception applies (e.g. Prison Intercepts).

In simple terms, a targeted interception warrant allows for the interception of a communication in the course of its transmission (e.g. traditional 'phone-tapping'). A targeted equipment interference warrant allows for interference with equipment to obtain communications data, where that data has been stored in the telecommunications system.

Section 56 provides a ban on the use of intercept material as evidence in court proceedings. It also prohibits the mention in court proceedings of anything, in any manner, which might infer that such an interception has occurred, may have occurred, or may be going to occur.

Schedule 3 provides a list of limited exceptions to section 56, one of which allows for the use of Prison Intercepts, and another allows for the use of evidence obtained with a Targeted Equipment Interference Warrant where the communication was stored in or by the telecommunications system.

USES

Intercept material provides investigators with direct, real-time access to conversations where criminals often speak openly and candidly about their activities. When used for intelligence purposes it assists with the detection and prevention of serious crime, and when used in court proceedings it can provide incredibly compelling evidence.

Where a service specifically designed for and advertised to criminals as private and confidential is then 'intercepted', the messages tend to be very revealing and provide a wealth of evidence to the authorities. This openness also means that attribution of a particular telephone number or username to an individual is fairly easy to do.

LIMITATIONS

Accessing and using this type of material is often resource-intensive, requiring significant technical expertise, manpower, and cross-jurisdictional cooperation. The legislation is also complex, resulting in time-consuming and expensive litigation about what material can and cannot be used evidentially.

PRESENTATION

When used evidentially, recorded telephone calls are usually packaged as a digital audio file with an accompanying written transcript. There is often a need to have the recordings translated, particularly with Foreign Intercepts. At trial, the audio recordings are often played through the OIC and the jury are provided with written copies of the transcripts so that they can follow along. These will need to be paginated, with some form of timestamp, paragraph numbering, or row numbering so that specific passages can be easily referred to.

When messages are used evidentially at trial, they are usually inserted into a 'working document' communications schedule. As discussed in an earlier chapter, these should have row numbering and be colour-coded (each individual should be assigned a unique colour).

Pre-trial, careful consideration needs to be given to disclosure. Once an investigation obtains this type of material it will need to be scheduled and then assessed for disclosure in the normal way – this is often resource intensive if hours of audio recordings need to be listened to. It is helpful for a specific disclosure strategy to be produced which sets out the practical arrangements for assessing the material.

PRISON INTERCEPTS

INTRODUCTION

One of the statutory exceptions in the IPA 2016 allows for the interception of communications inside prisons (as well as psychiatric hospitals and immigration detention centres). Prisons have private telecommunications systems that allow prisoners to maintain contact with others by telephone. Telephone calls made using these systems are recorded by the prison. Investigators are then able to obtain these recordings, for use both as intelligence and as evidence in court.

LAW AND GUIDANCE

Part 1 of the IPA 2016 sets out the general prohibition against interception and then various specific exceptions.

Sections 49 to 52 set out the relevant exceptions on "Interception taking place in certain institutions".

Section 49 specifically allows for interception in prisons, when it is done in accordance with the Prison Rules.

The Prison Rules 1999, Rule 35A (a similar provision is in The Young Offender Institution Rules 2000 at Rule 11) sets out very broad circumstances in which interception can be used.

Applying those broad rules (and following a direction from the Secretary of State), prisons implement a blanket recording policy on all social telecommunication calls. This policy is contained within the Authorised

Communications Controls and Interception Policy Framework, which justifies this approach as being necessary:

> *to allow for the retrospective identification and management of attempts to abuse the PIN phone system. Illicit communications can facilitate a range of criminality in both prisons and the community and will also impact on prisoners 'rehabilitative journeys. These communications cannot be identified in advance of being made because they can originate from any prisoner within the estate, and not solely those who are already subject to monitoring because of intelligence or risk assessments. Blanket interception also ensures that prisoners whose calls would otherwise not be intercepted are protected from coercive or threatening behaviour by those seeking to access their PIN-phone accounts. This is proportionate as prisoners and their social contacts are made aware that their calls are recorded and may be subject to monitoring. It is not however necessary to monitor most of these calls.*

Investigators can request access to the recordings, and the prison may release them under Rule 35C of The Prison Rules 1999 (or Rule 13 of The Young Offender Institution Rules 2000). It must both be necessary to release the material for a stated purpose, one of which is the prevention, detection, investigation, or prosecution of crime, and proportionate to do so.

Under the 'Authorised Communications Controls and Interception Policy Framework', any release can have handling arrangements applied to it. This can include a limit on the material being used evidentially.

FOREIGN
INTERCEPTS

INTRODUCTION

The prohibition on using intercept material as evidence only applies when the interception has been carried out in the UK. It does not apply to material obtained overseas by a foreign law enforcement authority and then provided to the UK authorities (provided the UK authorities have not initiated the intercept). Many other countries are perfectly happy to allow intercept material to be used in their prosecutions and to provide intercept material to law enforcement authorities in other jurisdictions.

Investigators in the UK are therefore able to use intercept material obtained overseas by foreign authorities, which can provide powerful evidence that would be entirely inadmissible if obtained in the UK.

LAW AND GUIDANCE

Section 3 of the IPA 2016, the provision making it a criminal offence to unlawfully intercept a communication, only applies to interception carried out in the UK. This means that the prohibition on using intercept material in court proceedings, contained in section 56, does not apply to material obtained by a foreign law enforcement authority.

R v Aujla [1998] 2 Cr App R 16 is one of the leading cases on this topic (although the court was considering an earlier statute, the principles and conclusions are also applicable to the IPA 2016). The Court of Appeal held that there was no prohibition in domestic law on the use, in evidence, of intercept material obtained by a foreign authority and then provided to a UK authority. The only question for the court was not of admissibility, but of the fairness in admitting the intercept evidence. Any application under section 78 of PACE 1984 to exclude the material would require consideration of the law in the foreign country (i.e. was the interception carried out in accordance with the domestic law in that jurisdiction?) and article 8 of the European Convention on Human Rights (i.e. had the individual's right to privacy been breached in an impermissible way?).

In another leading case of *R v P* [2000] UKHL 69, the House of Lords approved *R v Aujla* and found that the use of Foreign Intercepts did not necessarily breach either article 6 (right to a fair trial) or article 8 (right to respect for private and family life, home, and correspondence) of the European Convention on Human Rights.

The use of Foreign Intercepts as evidence is therefore governed by the normal principles of relevance and fairness, applied to the specific facts of the investigation.

It should also be noted that section 9 of the IPA 2016 prevents an investigator requesting a foreign authority to conduct interception unless an IPA warrant has been obtained. This is to prevent the UK authorities circumventing the prohibition on using intercept material in court proceedings by asking a foreign authority to carry out the interception instead.

ENCRYPTED
MESSAGING
INTERCEPTS

INTRODUCTION

A recent breakthrough in criminal investigations has been the ability to use, in evidence, messages exchanged through encrypted messaging services. Some of these services were specifically aimed at allowing organised crime groups to communicate without fear that law enforcement authorities would ever be able to obtain the messages. Although looking like traditional intercept material (which can be used for intelligence purposes but not evidentially), the courts have decided that these messages fall into a different category – but the issue is far from straightforward. The courts have had to grapple with very technical details of how modern telecommunication systems operate and how the messages have been obtained.

One such service was called EncroChat. It was advertised as being completely secure and ran on a specific type of mobile telephone provided by the operator. A user could only speak to another user if they knew their unique username (also known as a handle). Any communications or messages sent by the EncroChat mobile telephone were encrypted, transmitted, and then decrypted by the receiving mobile telephone so that it could be read.

In 2020, it became public knowledge that EncroChat had been compromised by European law enforcement agencies. The precise details of how this was achieved is not known as the information is protected by French secrecy laws, but the UK's National Crime Agency was then provided with messages from EncroChat users in the UK obtained during the operation. These messages showed that this particular service had been used to coordinate serious organised criminality involving violence, firearms, and drugs. Numerous criminal investigations and prosecutions followed, relying on the obtained messages as evidence.

Several years on, EncroChat prosecutions are still ongoing across the UK and other European jurisdictions. Other encrypted messaging services have sprung up hoping to replace and improve on EncroChat. Although this chapter focuses on that specific service, the legal and practical concepts will equally apply to other services targeted by law enforcement authorities in the future.

LAW AND GUIDANCE

In *R v A, B, D & C* [2021] EWCA Crim 128, the Court of Appeal had to decide if the trial judge had correctly admitted evidence obtained from the EncroChat infiltration. The material had been obtained in accordance with a Targeted Equipment Interference warrant granted under the IPA 2016.

The Court of Appeal set out the legal context of the issue it had to decide:

The 2016 Act adopted a domestic law framework which is unique in Europe and which resembles previous regimes. Historically, intercept material (classically phone tapping, but not limited to that) could be lawfully obtained by the authorities. Subject to a number of immaterial exceptions, it could not be used in evidence in proceedings but was reserved for intelligence use. The policy justification for that approach has been debated on many occasions and centres around protecting sensitive capabilities and wider operational and practical concerns. All were discussed in Intercept as Evidence, December 2014 Cmnd 8989 which was the report of a review of Privy Councillors provided to Ministers. In many other jurisdictions, including France and the Netherlands, there is no blanket prohibition on the admission into evidence of intercept material...

The essential point before us is the submission, rejected by the judge, that the EncroChat material is intercept material and inadmissible in criminal proceedings because of section 56 of the 2016 Act, and further that it was unlawfully obtained under a Targeted Equipment Interference warrant, when its obtaining should have been identified as a kind of interception which would require a Targeted Interception warrant. Targeted Equipment Interference warrants are governed by Part 5 of the 2016 Act and may produce material which can be used in evidence. Targeted Interception warrants are governed by Part 2 of the Act and the product is inadmissible in evidence in almost all criminal proceedings, including these. The judge found that the EncroChat material in this case was obtained under Part 5 warrants. These were approved by Sir Kenneth Parker, a Judicial Commissioner, on 5 March 2020, and Sir Brian Leveson, the Investigatory Powers Commissioner, on 26 March 2020, prior to the obtaining of the EncroChat material. The second warrant was needed in order to widen the scope of the first for reasons which are not material to the issues before us. The issue is whether that approach was correct, or whether on a true understanding of the way the data were obtained, and of the 2016 Act, they comprised material obtained unlawfully under the wrong warrant and, in any event, were inadmissible…

After a careful and detailed analysis of the statutory regime, the Court summarised the position:

The task of the court, as the judge correctly said, is to understand the system and then to decide whether, as a matter of ordinary language, the communication was being transmitted or stored at the time of extraction. If the former, it is inadmissible. If the latter, it is admissible, provided the appropriate warrant was in place.

The Court reasoned that:

The policy of the 2016 Act is that all conduct caught within the section 4 definition should be criminal, unless done lawfully under an appropriate warrant and by an appropriate person. This includes an act whose effect is to make content of communications available to a third party both "while the communication is being transmitted" (section 4(4)(a)) and "any time when" it "is stored in or by the system" (section 4(4)(b)). However, as we have seen, in relation to "stored" communications a different policy as to secrecy applies. There is no necessary connection between these two policies. An act may be criminalised, and its nature and product may also be protected from disclosure, or it may be criminalised and there need be no such protection. These are policy decisions for Parliament...

The answer to this appeal is found in the construction of section 4(1) and (4)(4)(b) of the 2016 Act. Section 4(4)(b), read beside section 4(1)(b), means that a message which is, for example, monitored while it is stored in or by the system by means of which it is transmitted is intercepted while it is in the course of transmission...

The structure of section 4(4) is important here. The conjunction which connects section 4(4)(a) and 4(4)(b) is "and" not "or". The appellants' submission that the court must start with section 4(4)(a) and determine whether a message was intercepted while being transmitted and, if the answer to that is yes, cannot then go on to consider whether it was also, at the same time, being stored is simply wrong. The words in the parenthesis of section 4(4)(b) do not require that conclusion. They simply mean that it does not matter whether the storage began before or after the transmission. It is unnecessary to add any words there to catch storage while the communication is being transmitted because that is necessarily caught by the plain words of the provision...

As a matter of ordinary language, section 4(4)(b) is clear and unambiguous in its meaning. It extends to all communications which are stored on the system, whenever that might occur. That broad meaning coheres with the structure of the 2016 Act considered in overview, and importantly with the different types of warrantry for which the Act provides. Part 5 warrants are required for the interception of stored material, and Part 2 warrants for material which is to be intercepted while being transmitted.

Applying the law to the specific facts of EncroChat, the Court decided that:

The statutory question for any court in determining if section 4(4)(b) applies is this: was the communication stored in or by the system at the time when it was intercepted? The judge's findings of fact are set out above. He found that the communications were extracted directly from the handset of the user and not while they were travelling to, through or from any other part of the system. This is a process which is like any other means of downloading the content of a mobile phone handset. It is done remotely, but it is done by interrogating the RAM of the phone, not by intercepting the communication after it has left the phone. In the case of the sender the material was recovered in the form of unencrypted messages stored in the RAM of the device in a form in which they existed before they were transmitted from the device to the servers in Roubaix, via the telecommunications system. This provides the answer to the statutory question. The material was stored when it was intercepted. It was within section 4(4)(b).

The Court of Appeal therefore upheld the use of the material extracted from EncroChat, on the basis that it was material intercepted directly from the storage on the mobile telephones and not taken in the course of transmission.

Despite this judgment, as of February 2023 there remains ongoing litigation challenging the admissibility of EncroChat material. At least one further case has been decided by the Court of Appeal (currently under a reporting restriction), and the Investigatory Powers Tribunal (IPT) is considering the legality of the warrants used in all of the EncroChat cases (warrants under the IPA 2016 are covered in more detail in a separate chapter). There are reports of EncroChat cases now before both the European Court of Human Rights and the Court of Justice of the European Union.

FUTURE DEVELOPMENTS

There are ongoing appeals (and other litigation) relating to the admissibility of EncroChat material. Further judgments are likely in the near future.

It is also likely that new encrypted messaging services will spring up as older ones are infiltrated by law enforcement authorities. The game of 'whack-a-mole' will continue.

PART TWO

NOTICES

AND

WARRANTS

SECTION 49
RIPA NOTICES

Given that modern mobile telephones and computers have built-in encryption, switched on by default, it has become more difficult for investigators to gain access to the data they contain. As discussed in the chapter on Mobile Telephone Extraction, many encrypted devices can still be accessed using specialist software, but this is resource-intensive and device-specific.

The most straightforward solution is to simply ask the owner of the device for the password (the 'key' to decrypt the data). The Regulation of Investigatory Powers Act 2000 (RIPA) provides a formal procedure for this, backed up with criminal sanctions if a request is then refused.

Section 49 requires an investigator to have lawfully obtained electronic information which cannot be accessed or put into an intelligible form without a key (usually a password), and there are reasonable grounds to believe: (a) that an individual is in possession of that key; (b) that it is necessary to obtain the electronic information for one of the stated purposes, which includes to prevent or detect crime; (c) that the imposition of the notice would be proportionate; and (d) that is it not reasonably practicable to obtain the electronic information in another way.

Permission to serve a section 49 notice, which is the formal request to disclose the key, must then be sought from an appropriately ranked officer within the investigator's organisation or from a Circuit Judge (Schedule 2 sets out who can grant permission). A written notice is then served on the individual believed to have the key, which sets out the details of the request and states the time by which it must be complied with (this must be reasonable in all the circumstances).

Section 53 makes it a criminal offence, triable either summarily or on indictment, to knowingly fail to comply with a section 49 notice. The maximum sentence depends on the type of material believed to be on the encrypted device – if national security or child indecency then the maximum is 5 years' imprisonment and in any other case is it 2 years' imprisonment.

It should be noted that the use of formal section 49 notices is quite rare. It is far more common for investigators to issue 'advisory' notices, which are informal documents essentially stating that they intend to seek permission to serve a section 49 notice unless the requested key is voluntarily disclosed.

TARGETED INTERCEPTION WARRANTS

The provisions relating to targeted interception warrants are contained within Part 2 of the IPA 2016. There is an accompanying 'Interception of Communications Code of Practice' which provides guidance on their use.

These warrants provide the lawful authority to intercept a communication in the course of its transmission (e.g. traditional 'phone-tapping'). Section 18 contains a list of organisations that can apply to the Secretary of State for such a warrant, and the application can only be granted if necessary for one of the stated purposes which include the prevention and detection of serious crime.

Section 263 defines "serious crime" as:

> *(a) the offence, or one of the offences, which is or would be constituted by the conduct concerned is an offence for which a person who has reached the age of 18 (or, in relation to Scotland or Northern Ireland, 21) and has no previous convictions could reasonably be expected to be sentenced to imprisonment for a term of 3 years or more, or (b) the conduct involves the use of violence, results in substantial financial gain or is conduct by a large number of persons in pursuit of a common purpose*

The grant of a warrant is then reviewed by a Judicial Commissioner, applying the same principles as would be applied by a court on an application for judicial review. The decision to grant a warrant is then either approved or refused.

Material obtained using these warrants is for intelligence-purposes only. Section 56 provides a ban on its use as evidence in court proceedings. It also prohibits the mention in court proceedings of anything, in any manner, which might infer that such an interception has occurred, may have occurred, or may be going to occur.

TARGETED
EQUIPMENT
INTERFERENCE
WARRANTS

The provisions relating to targeted equipment interference warrants are contained within Part 5 of the IPA 2016. There is an accompanying 'Equipment Interference Code of Practice' which provides guidance on their use.

These warrants provide the lawful authority to interfere with equipment to obtain communications data. The guidance provides the following examples of when such a warrant may be used:

> *Equipment interference operations vary in complexity. At the lower end of the complexity scale, an equipment interference authority may covertly download data from a subject's mobile device when it is left unattended, or an equipment interference authority may use someone's login credentials to gain access to data held on a computer. More complex equipment interference operations may involve exploiting existing vulnerabilities in software in order to gain control of devices or networks to remotely extract material or monitor the user of the device.*

Sections 102 to 107 contains various powers to issue this sort of warrant. In general, an appropriately ranked officer within an investigator's organisation can issue a warrant provided that a Judicial Commissioner has approved the decision. A warrant must be necessary to prevent or detect serious crime.

Section 263 defines "serious crime" as:

(a) the offence, or one of the offences, which is or would be constituted by the conduct concerned is an offence for which a person who has reached the age of 18 (or, in relation to Scotland or Northern Ireland, 21) and has no previous convictions could reasonably be expected to be sentenced to imprisonment for a term of 3 years or more, or (b) the conduct involves the use of violence, results in substantial financial gain or is conduct by a large number of persons in pursuit of a common purpose

Material obtained using these warrants is not covered by the section 56 prohibition on the use of intercept material in court proceedings, and so can be used for evidential purposes.

PART THREE

DISCLOSURE

MANAGING
DISCLOSURE

INTRODUCTION

One of the key issues in any modern criminal investigation is disclosure, made more difficult by the sheer volume of digital communications evidence now collected by investigators. It is crucial that such evidence is properly retained, scheduled, and reviewed – but it is also important that decisions about disclosure are recorded and explained so that all parties involved in a case can understand what has and has not been done.

This chapter summarises the law and guidance on disclosure, and then discusses the key methods used to manage the disclosure of digital communications evidence.

LAW AND GUIDANCE

The disclosure test in criminal proceedings is set out in section 3 of the Criminal Procedure and Investigations Act 1996 (CPIA). It places a duty on a prosecutor to:

> *disclose to the accused any prosecution material which has not previously been disclosed to the accused and which might reasonably be considered capable of undermining the case for the prosecution against the accused or of assisting the case for the accused*

Guidance is provided in the 'CPIA Code of Practice'. It sets out the general disclosure responsibilities of those involved in a criminal investigation.

The Crown Prosecution Service has also published: (a) a 'Disclosure Manual', which provides general instructions on how disclosure should be carried out and specific instructions on digital media in Chapter 30; (b) 'Disclosure – A guide to "reasonable lines of enquiry" and communications evidence', which provides guidance on Mobile Telephone Extraction; and (c) 'Disclosure – Guidelines on Communications Evidence', which provides guidance on communications generally.

Further guidance is provided in the 'Attorney General's Guidelines on Disclosure'. These provide "high-level principles which should be followed when the disclosure regime is applied throughout England and Wales", but they also give specific, detailed guidance for digital media (including digital communications evidence). Annex A sets out: general principles that should be applied by investigators; how digital devices should be seized and retained; how digital material believed to be covered by legal professional privilege should be dealt with; and how digital material should be examined, recorded, and scheduled.

Regarding the extent of examination required, which is often an area of confusion and dispute, Annex A states that:

> It is important for investigators and prosecutors to remember that the duty under the CPIA Code is to "pursue all reasonable lines of inquiry including those that point away from the suspect".

> Lines of inquiry, of whatever kind, should be pursued only if they are reasonable in the context of the individual case. It is not the duty of the prosecution to comb through all the material in its possession (e.g. every word or byte of computer material) on the lookout for anything which might conceivably or speculatively undermine the case or assist the defence. The duty of the prosecution is to disclose material which might reasonably be considered capable of undermining its case or assisting the case for the accused which they become aware of, or to which their attention is drawn.

That section goes on to list various tools available to investigators to aid with the examination process – this is discussed in a later chapter.

SPECIFIC DISCLOSURE STRATEGIES

In large criminal investigations, it is important for the disclosure of digital communications evidence to be closely managed from the outset. This is usually done using specific disclosure strategies that cover a particular type of evidence and are closely tailored to the investigation. These documents set out the material already collected (and likely to be collected) and set out the investigation's approach to disclosure – how that material will be reviewed, any known defences and issues raised, and the items that are likely to meet the disclosure test.

Annex A of the 'Attorney General's Guidelines on Disclosure' supports this approach, stating that:

> *In cases involving very large quantities of data, the person in charge of the investigation will develop a strategy setting out how the material should be analysed or searched to identify categories of data. This strategy may include an initial scoping exercise of the material obtained to ascertain the most effective strategy for reviewing relevant material...*

> *Where search terms are to be used, investigators and prosecutors should consider whether engagement with the defence at the pre-charge stage would assist in the identification of relevant search terms. It will usually be appropriate to provide to the accused and their legal representative with a copy of the reasonable search terms used, or to be used, and to invite them to suggest any further reasonable search terms. If search terms are suggested which the investigator or prosecutor believes will not be productive, for example where the use of common words is likely to identify a mass of irrelevant material,*

the investigator or prosecutor should discuss the issues with the defence in order to agree sensible refinements...

One type of evidence that often requires a specific strategy is Mobile Telephone Extraction. A strategy document will set out all the mobile telephones that have been seized and will record the level of extraction intended for each (with the justification for why that level of extraction has been selected). A reviewing strategy will then identify what sort of material is likely to be relevant (e.g. call logs, SMS text messages, photos, videos), how that material will be reviewed (e.g. manually, keyword searches), and what items within that material are likely to meet the disclosure test (e.g. SMS text messages containing drug terms, telephone calls with identified telephone numbers).

Another type of evidence requiring a specific strategy is admissible intercept material (including Prison Intercepts and Foreign Intercepts). A strategy document will identify the intercepts that have been obtained, where they have been obtained from, whether they will need to be translated, how they will be reviewed (e.g. manually, keyword searches), and which specific individuals, topics, phrases, or words are likely to meet the disclosure test.

Subject to anything sensitive that might need to be removed, these strategies can then be appended to a DMD once the case has reached that stage. This ensures that the court and the defence understand the disclosure process and can have confidence that it has been carried out thoroughly.

DISCLOSURE MANAGEMENT DOCUMENTS

A DMD is a written document used at the prosecution stage to outline the strategy and approach taken in relation to disclosure. DMDs are now mandatory in all Crown Court cases and should be considered for cases in the Magistrates' Court and Youth Court.

The CPS 'Disclosure Manual' sets out what a DMD should contain:

1. *How the disclosure responsibilities have been managed;*

2. *A brief summary of the prosecution case and a statement outlining how the prosecutor's approach complies with the disclosure regime;*

3. *The prosecutor's understanding of the defence case, including information revealed during interview. The prosecutor may wish to explain their understanding of what is in dispute and what is not in dispute, the lines of inquiry that have been pursued as a result of these issues and specific disclosure decisions that have been taken;*

4. *An outline of the prosecutor's approach to disclosure, including:*

   1. *The lines of inquiry pursued, particularly those which may assist the defence.*

   2. *The timescales for disclosure and, where relevant, how the review of unused material has been prioritised.*

   3. *The method and extent of examination of digital material, in accordance with the Annex A to the AG's Guidelines.*

4.   *Any potential video footage.*

5.   *Any linked investigations, including an explanation of the nexus between investigations and any memoranda of understanding and disclosure agreements between investigators.*

6.   *Any third-party material, including the steps taken to obtain the material.*

7.   *Any international material, including the steps taken to obtain the material.*

8.   *Credibility of prosecution witnesses (including professional witnesses).*

Of note are the references to digital material and the 'Attorney General's Guidelines on Disclosure'. Annex A of those Guidelines provides guidance on the use of a DMD:

In cases involving very large quantities of data, the person in charge of the investigation will develop a strategy setting out how the material should be analysed or searched to identify categories of data. This strategy may include an initial scoping exercise of the material obtained to ascertain the most effective strategy for reviewing relevant material. Any such strategy should be agreed with the prosecutor and communicated to the court and defence using a DMD…

The digital strategy must be set out in an IMD [an Investigation Management Document – a document provided by the investigator to the prosecutor so that a DMD can be drafted] and subsequently a DMD. This should include the details of any sampling techniques used (including key word searches) and how the material identified as a result was examined…

Annex C of those Guidelines provide a template DMD, which includes a section on electronic material, stating:

This section should cover the following issues:

What mobile telephones/communication devices/computers were seized during the investigation (from all suspects, complainants, witnesses).

Identify the items with reference to the schedule of materials – i.e. telephone, download

Have the devices been downloaded? If not, why not. If so, what type of download?

Set out the method of examination of each download – were key words deployed, was the entire download inspected, were date parameters employed?

What social media accounts of suspect/complaint/witness have been considered a reasonable line of inquiry.

Were any phones from the complainant or suspect not seized? If not, why not?

Set out the method by which the defence will be given disclosure of material that satisfies the disclosure test explaining, if relevant, why the whole item is not being provided.

What CCTV/multi-media evidence has been seized and how it has been examined?

A table is then provided which gives the suggested format for presenting the above information. For each exhibit identified, it lists the description, inquiry undertaken, and result.

When drafting a DMD, it is particularly important that the information contained within such a table is precise, accurate, and detailed. Where the inquiry undertaken is Mobile Telephone Extraction, the DMD needs to record the level of extraction carried out, the precise method of extraction (e.g. what brand of extraction software was used), the types of data extracted (e.g. call logs, SMS text messages, contacts, photographs, videos), which of those types were reviewed and how, and which of those types were not reviewed and why. The results section of the table needs to identify what material was served as evidence (in what format) and what unused material was disclosed (in what format). The use of terms such as 'full download' or 'raw data' should be avoided, as they lack precision.

The DMD is referred to as a 'living document', which means that it can and should be updated as a prosecution progresses.

DISCLOSURE
TOOLS

INTRODUCTION

This chapter discusses some of the tools that can be used by investigators to examine large quantities of digital communications evidence. These are required in cases where a manual review of each item would be unreasonable or disproportionate.

In the leading case of *R v R* [2015] EWCA Crim 1941, the Court of Appeal approved the use of such tools, stating:

> *... In our judgment, it has been clear for some time that the prosecution is not required to do the impossible, nor should the duty of giving initial disclosure be rendered incapable of fulfilment through the physical impossibility of reading (and scheduling) each and every item of material seized; common sense must be applied. In such circumstances, the prosecution is entitled to use appropriate sampling and search terms and its record-keeping and scheduling obligations are modified accordingly...*

> *... The extent of the duty imposed on the prosecution at this stage, while obviously fact specific, must take account that it is initial disclosure with which the prosecution is then concerned. The right course at the stage of initial disclosure is for the prosecution to formulate a disclosure strategy, canvass that strategy with the Court and the defence and to utilise technology to make an appropriate search or conduct an appropriate sampling exercise of the material seized...*

As discussed in an earlier chapter, drafting a specific disclosure strategy is important so that the task of disclosure can be shaped and planned at an early stage – this includes identifying any tools that will be used and any specific parameters that will need to be applied. This requires engagement with the defence at all stages. Transparency is required so that the defence know what is and is not being done, and so that they have an opportunity to comment on the process.

KEYWORD SEARCHES

Keyword searching uses software to search through the material and automatically flag up any items that contain pre-identified phrases or words. More advanced searches can be applied which require multiple words or phrases to be present in a document before it is flagged up, and other parameters can also be applied to narrow the search down further (e.g. date and timestamps). The identified documents are then manually reviewed to assess if they meet the disclosure test.

It is important for all parties to consider both the keywords that will be applied and how the software will apply them (e.g. it is crucial to know if the searches will be case-sensitive and how the software will deal with like-words).

Guidance on the use of keyword searches is contained within the CPS 'Disclosure Manual: Annex D – The Use of Keyword Searches and Digital Evidence Recovery Officers'.

DOCUMENT REVIEW

Disclosure counsel are often instructed in large investigations, where lots of material might need to be manually reviewed. A guidance document is usually produced, setting out the categories of material included in the review and how the disclosure test should be applied to them. This is done to achieve consistency, but peer-review, multiple levels of reviews, and dip-sampling checks are often also used to ensure that the review is thorough and reliable.

The review is usually carried out with special review software. Material is loaded onto the software, which disclosure counsel then use to read the documents and record decisions they make about them. The software then categorises the material, allowing for the relevant documents to be scheduled and the disclosable material to be packaged for service on the defence.

ARTIFICIAL INTELLIGENCE AND MACHINE LEARNING

An emerging technology in disclosure is the use of artificial intelligence (AI) and machine learning. This uses specialist software to read, analyse, and then actually make decisions about documents that disclosure counsel might otherwise be used to make. The process requires lawyers and software developers to design the initial search terms. The software then works through documents very quickly, improving its own algorithms and learning from any mistakes it makes as it goes. The point is that the software does not just blindly identify documents for later review but makes judgements about them.

Despite on its face appearing to be a neat solution to the disclosure problems facing modern investigations, there are several issues with the use of AI. Firstly, it is an emerging technology. This makes it both very expensive and susceptible to errors. It might therefore make more sense for it to be refined outside of the criminal justice system first (i.e. in an area where a failure does not have such serious consequences). Secondly, AI tends to be poor at explaining why a decision has been reached. For example, the document read by the software and the disclosure decision made will both be known – but the reasons why the software has made that particular decision might not be. It is difficult to see how this complies with the obligations on prosecutors to explain how disclosure decisions have been reached. Finally, it is not clear-cut that the law allows for decisions to be delegated to technology in this way. It is one thing for a lawyer to make the final decision to disclose material, having had software identify it through a keyword search. It is entirely another thing for the software to actually make the final decision. The CPIA and the various supporting guidance documents all assume a human will ultimately be discharging disclosure obligations.

COMPLAINANTS – MOBILE TELEPHONE EXTRACTION

INTRODUCTION

This chapter addresses the specific issue of complainants and how evidence of their communications should be dealt with during a criminal investigation, given the potential tension between a complainant's right to privacy and the duty on an investigator to pursue all reasonable lines of inquiry. In the last few years, concerns have been raised by both the Information Commissioner and the Victims' Commissioner that this tension was often being inappropriately resolved by a complainant having their mobile telephone taken, retained for long periods, and subjected to in-depth review. Following various reviews and reports, in 2022 the government brought in new legislation to put the taking of a mobile telephone from a complainant or a witness on a statutory footing.

STATUTORY POWERS

In addition to the coercive powers to seize a mobile telephone from a suspect (covered in the chapter on Mobile Telephone Extraction), an investigator now has a statutory power to request that a complainant or a witness voluntarily hand over their mobile telephone for examination. This power is contained in Chapter 3 of Part 2 of the Police, Crime, Sentencing and Courts Act 2022.

Section 37 of that Act allows for an investigator to carry out Mobile Telephone Extraction on a mobile telephone that has been voluntarily provided to them, where that user has agreed that information can be extracted from it. The power can only be exercised if the data extraction is necessary for one of the stated purposes, which includes for the prevention, detection, investigation, and prosecution of crime. The investigator must reasonably believe that information stored on the device is relevant to a reasonable line of enquiry which is being pursued. The investigator must also have regard to the 'Extraction of information from electronic devices: code of practice', which contains guidance on how the power should be applied.

Section 39 sets out specific requirements that must be met for the mobile telephone to have been 'voluntarily' provided and for the user to have agreed that information can be extracted from it. An investigator must not place undue pressure on the user to provide the device or agree to extraction, and the user must be provided with a written notice setting out what information is sought, why it is sought, how the information will be dealt with, that the user may refuse, and that the investigation will not be brought to an end merely because the user refuses to provide the device or agree to extraction.

R V BATER-JAMES

It is important for that statutory power and guidance to be considered in the context of the leading case of *R v Bater-James* [2020] EWCA Crim 790. The first paragraph of that judgment summarises the issues the court had to address:

> *These two otherwise unrelated cases have been listed together to provide the court an opportunity to consider various issues relating to the retention, inspection, copying, disclosure and deletion of the electronic records held by prosecution witnesses. These issues frequently arise in the context of sexual offences as regards material stored on complainants' mobile telephones, but they occur in a wide range of other circumstances. Therefore, although this judgment focusses on the position of complainants who allege sexual*

impropriety, the principles will be equally relevant – depending always on the facts – to other prosecution witnesses. For these reasons we have used the words "complainant" and "witness" interchangeably.

The Court of Appeal went on to set out four frequently-arising issues of principle in cases where a complainant's mobile telephone might need to be examined:

The First Issue of Principle

Identifying the circumstances when it is necessary for investigators to seek details of a witness's digital communications. These are usually, but by no means always, electronic exchanges conducted by way of multiple platforms on smart mobile telephones, tablets or computers. These platforms are so numerous that it is pointless to attempt to list examples. In essence, the question in this context is when does it become necessary to attempt to review a witness's digitally stored communications? The linked question is when is it necessary to disclose digital communications to which the investigators have access?

The Second Issue of Principle

When it is necessary, how should the review of the witness's electronic communications be conducted?

The Third Issue of Principle

What reassurance should be provided to the complainant as to ambit of the review and the circumstances of any disclosure of material that is relevant to the case?

The Fourth Issue of Principle

What is the consequence if the complainant refuses to permit access to a potentially relevant device, either by way of "downloading" the contents (in reality, copying) or permitting an officer to view parts of the device (including, inter alia, copying some material, for instance by taking "screen shots")? Similarly, what are the consequences if the complainant deletes relevant material?

The Court of Appeal then answered each question as follows:

... In conclusion on the first issue, and answering the question: "when does it become necessary to attempt to review a witness's digitally-stored communications and when is it necessary to disclose digital communications to which the investigators have access?", we stress that regardless of the medium in which the information is held, a 'reasonable line of enquiry' will depend on the facts of, and the issues in, the individual case, including any potential defence. There is no presumption that a complainant's mobile telephone or other devices should be inspected, retained or downloaded, any more than there is a presumption that investigators will attempt to look through material held in hard copy. There must be a properly identifiable foundation for the inquiry, not mere conjecture or speculation. Furthermore, as developed below, if there is a reasonable line of enquiry, the investigators should consider whether there are ways of readily accessing the information that do not involve looking at or taking possession of the complainant's mobile telephone or other digital device. Disclosure should only occur when the material might reasonably be considered capable of undermining the prosecution's case or assisting the case for the accused...

... In conclusion on the second issue and answering the question: "how should the review of the witness's electronic communications be conducted?", investigators will need to adopt an incremental approach. First, to consider with care the nature and detail of any review that is required, the particular areas that need to be looked at and whether this can happen without recourse to the complainant's mobile telephone or other device. Second, and only if it is necessary to look at the complainant's digital device or devices, a critical question is whether it is sufficient simply to view limited areas (e.g. an

identified string of messages/emails or particular postings on social media). In some cases, this will be achieved by simply looking at the relevant material and taking screenshots or making some other record, without taking possession of, or copying, the device. Third, if a more extensive enquiry is necessary, the contents of the device should be downloaded with the minimum inconvenience to the complainant and, if possible, it should be returned without any unnecessary delay. If the material is voluminous, consideration should be given to appropriately focussed enquiries using search terms, a process in which the defendant should participate. It may be possible to apply data parameters to any search. Finally, appropriate redactions should be made to any disclosed material to avoid revealing irrelevant personal information...

... In conclusion on the third issue and answering the question: "what reassurance should be provided to the complainant?", the complainant should be told i) that the prosecution will keep him or her informed as to any decisions that are made as to disclosure, including how long the investigators will keep the device; what it is planned to be "extracted" from it by copying; and what thereafter is to be "examined", potentially leading to disclosure; ii) that in any event, any content within the mobile telephone or other device will only be copied or inspected if there is no other appropriate method of discharging the prosecution's disclosure obligations; and iii) material will only be provided to the defence if it meets the strict test for disclosure and it will be served in a suitably redacted form to ensure that personal details or other irrelevant information are not unnecessarily revealed (e.g. photographs, addresses or full telephone numbers)...

... In conclusion on the fourth issue and answering the question: "what is the consequence if the complainant refuses to permit access to a potentially relevant device or if the complainant deletes relevant material?", it is important to look carefully at the reasons for a refusal to permit access and to furnish the witness with an explanation and reassurance as to the procedure that will be followed if the device is

made available to the investigator. If it is suggested that the proceedings should be stayed, the court will need to consider the adequacy of the trial process, and whether this will ensure there is fairness to the defendant, particularly by way of cross-examination of the witness, coupled with appropriate judicial directions. The court should not be drawn into guessing at the content and significance of the material that may have become unavailable. Instead, the court must assess the impact of the absence of the particular missing evidence and whether the trial process can sufficiently compensate for its absence. An application can be made for a witness summons for the mobile telephone or other device to be produced. If the witness deletes material, although each case will need to be assessed on its own facts, we stress the potential utility of cross-examination and carefully crafted judicial directions. If the proceedings are not stayed and the trial proceeds, the uncooperative stance by the witness, investigated by appropriate questioning, will be an important factor that the jury will be directed to take into account when deciding, first, whether to accept the evidence of the witness and, second, whether they are sure of the defendant's guilt...

Investigators must therefore carefully apply the above principles whenever they are considering asking a complainant or a witness to hand over their mobile telephone. If they conclude that it is a reasonable line of inquiry, then they will need to consider Section 37 of the Police, Crime, Sentencing and Courts Act 2022 and the 'Extraction of information from electronic devices: code of practice'.

As stated above, section 39 requires a complainant or witness to be told that an investigation will not end merely because they refuse to hand over their mobile telephone. The Court of Appeal in *R v Bater-James* has set out how any subsequent prosecution will not necessarily be stayed because of such a refusal – the court will instead need to consider whether the trial process can sufficiently compensate.

MORE BOOKS BY
LAW BRIEF PUBLISHING

A selection of our other titles available now:-

'A Practical Guide to Parental Alienation in Private and Public Law Children Cases' by Sam King QC & Frankie Shama
'Contested Heritage – Removing Art from Land and Historic Buildings' by Richard Harwood QC, Catherine Dobson, David Sawtell
'The Limits of Separate Legal Personality: When Those Running a Company Can Be Held Personally Liable for Losses Caused to Third Parties Outside of the Company' by Dr Mike Wilkinson
'A Practical Guide to Transgender Law' by Robin Moira White & Nicola Newbegin
'Artificial Intelligence – The Practical Legal Issues (2nd Edition)' by John Buyers
'A Practical Guide to Residential Freehold Conveyancing' by Lorraine Richardson
'A Practical Guide to Pensions on Divorce for Lawyers' by Bryan Scant
'A Practical Guide to Challenging Sham Marriage Allegations in Immigration Law' by Priya Solanki
'A Practical Guide to Legal Rights in Scotland' by Sarah-Jane Macdonald
'A Practical Guide to New Build Conveyancing' by Paul Sams & Rebecca East
'A Practical Guide to Defending Barristers in Disciplinary Cases' by Marc Beaumont
'A Practical Guide to Inherited Wealth on Divorce' by Hayley Trim
'A Practical Guide to Practice Direction 12J and Domestic Abuse in Private Law Children Proceedings' by Rebecca Cross & Malvika Jaganmohan
'A Practical Guide to Confiscation and Restraint' by Narita Bahra QC, John Carl Townsend, David Winch
'A Practical Guide to the Law of Forests in Scotland' by Philip Buchan
'A Practical Guide to Health and Medical Cases in Immigration Law' by Rebecca Chapman & Miranda Butler
'A Practical Guide to Bad Character Evidence for Criminal Practitioners by Aparna Rao
'A Practical Guide to Extradition Law post-Brexit' by Myles Grandison et al

These books and more are available to order online direct from the publisher at www.lawbriefpublishing.com, where you can also read free sample chapters. For any queries, contact us on 0844 587 2383 or mail@lawbriefpublishing.com.

Our books are also usually in stock at www.amazon.co.uk with free next day delivery for Prime members, and at good legal bookshops such as Wildy & Sons.

We are regularly launching new books in our series of practical day-to-day practitioners' guides. Visit our website and join our free newsletter to be kept informed and to receive special offers, free chapters, etc.

You can also follow us on Twitter at www.twitter.com/lawbriefpub.

Milton Keynes UK
Ingram Content Group UK Ltd.
UKHW011004150324
439468UK00005B/415